WHAT DOES A STATE LEGISLATURE DO?

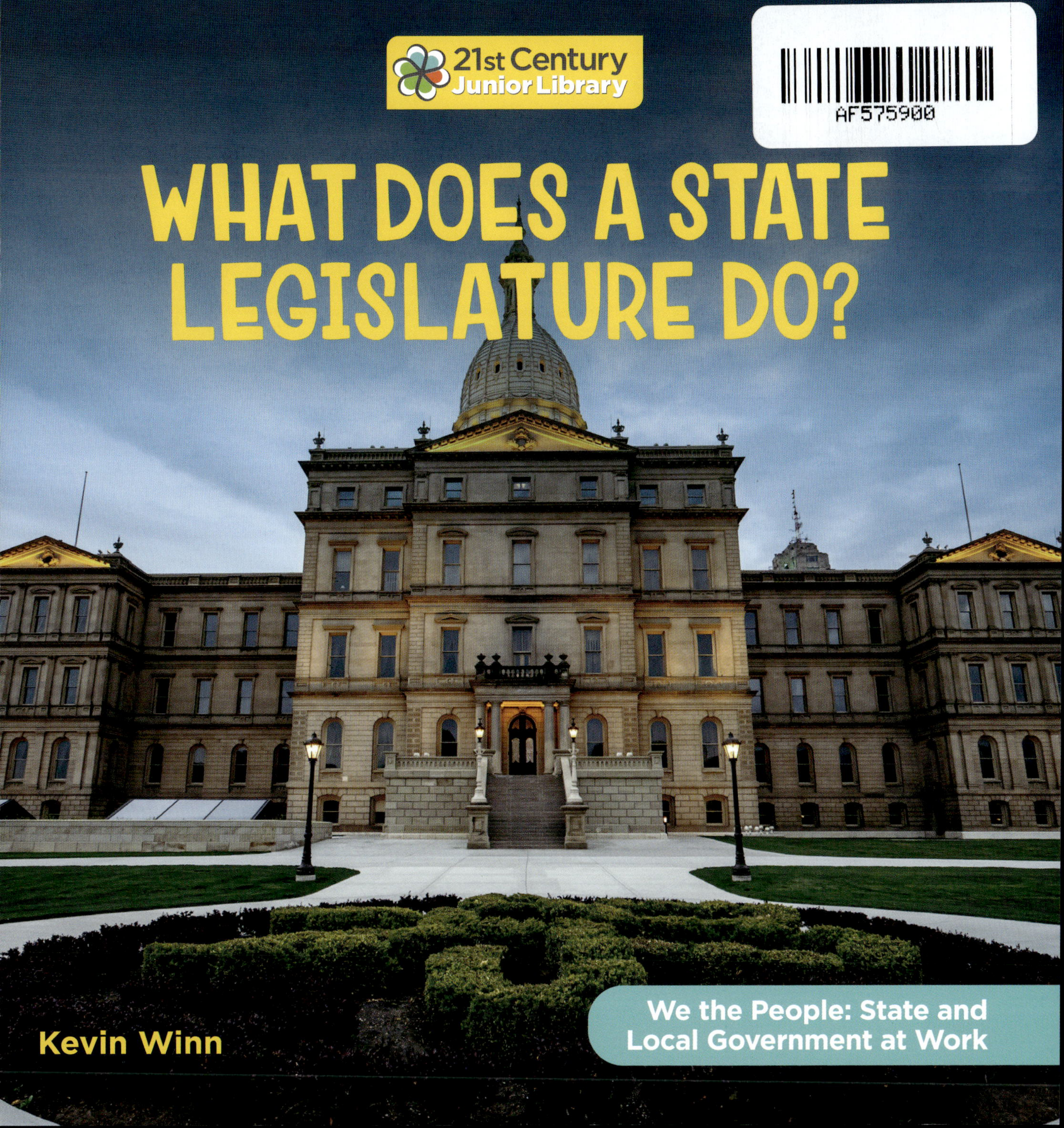

Kevin Winn

We the People: State and Local Government at Work

Published in the United States of America by:

CHERRY LAKE PRESS
2395 South Huron Parkway, Suite 200, Ann Arbor, Michigan 48104
www.cherrylakepress.com

Reading Adviser: Beth Walker Gambro, MS, Ed., Reading Consultant, Yorkville, IL
Content Adviser: Mark Richards, Ph.D., Professor, Dept. of Political Science, Grand Valley State University, Allendale, MI

Photo Credits: © RebeccaDLev/Shutterstock, cover, title page; © JC Gonram/Shutterstock, 5; © Sherry V Smith/Shutterstock, 6; create jobs 51/Shutterstock, 7; © Mircea Moira/Shutterstock, 9; © Maxx-Studio/Shutterstock, 9; © JackKPhoto/Shutterstock, 10–11; © Jason Finn/Shutterstock, 13; © Dennis MacDonald/Shutterstock, 13; © Dennis MacDonald/Shutterstock, 14; © LouiesWorld1/Shutterstock, 16; © Monkey Business Images/Shutterstock, 19; © fizkes/Shutterstock, 20; © Paul Brady Photography/Shutterstock, 21

Copyright © 2025 by Cherry Lake Publishing Group

All rights reserved. No part of this book may be reproduced or utilized in any form or by any means without written permission from the publisher.

Cherry Lake Press is an imprint of Cherry Lake Publishing Group.

Library of Congress Cataloging-in-Publication Data has been filed and is available at catalog.loc.gov.

Cherry Lake Press would like to acknowledge the work of the Partnership for 21st Century Learning, a Network of Battelle for Kids. Please visit Battelle for Kids online for more information.

Printed in the United States of America

Note from publisher: Websites change regularly, and their future contents are outside of our control. Supervise children when conducting any recommended online searches for extended learning opportunities.

CONTENTS

WHAT IS A STATE LEGISLATURE?

The United States of America has different levels of government. The country has a national government. Each state also has its own government.

State governments work in their state's capital city. Some state capitol buildings are hundreds of years old.

Just like the national government, there are three branches of government in each state:

1. Legislature: The **legislative** branch makes the laws.
2 Governor: The **executive** branch makes sure people follow the laws.
3. Courts: The **judicial** branch decides how to understand and apply the laws.

The U.S. Capitol building in Washington, D.C., is where the nation's legislature works.

State lawmakers each have a staff of people that work with them to serve the people of their state.

Like the U.S. Congress, the state legislature is a group of people who write laws and make them official. In some states, the state legislature is called the General **Assembly**. Massachusetts calls it the General Court.

Passing a law is not a simple process. When someone has an idea for a new law, it's called a bill. The bill first goes to a committee. This is a small group of **legislators**. They decide if the bill should be voted on by the whole legislature.

If the bill passes from the committee, all the legislators can talk about it. Some may want the bill to pass. Others may not. They talk about their reasons. This is called a **debate**. At this stage, the bill can be **amended**, or changed. If enough lawmakers agree, they vote for the bill. But a bill may die at any time if not enough lawmakers support it.

Create!

Anyone can suggest a bill and ask the state legislature to vote for it. What is a law that you think your state should pass? Write a paragraph about your new law. Give two reasons why this law would be helpful.

In most states, the governor must sign the bill for it to become a law. So even if the legislature approves a bill, the governor can decide to reject it through a **veto**. It is possible for the lawmakers to **override** this veto, but it's difficult. It takes more votes to override a veto than it did to pass the bill the first time.

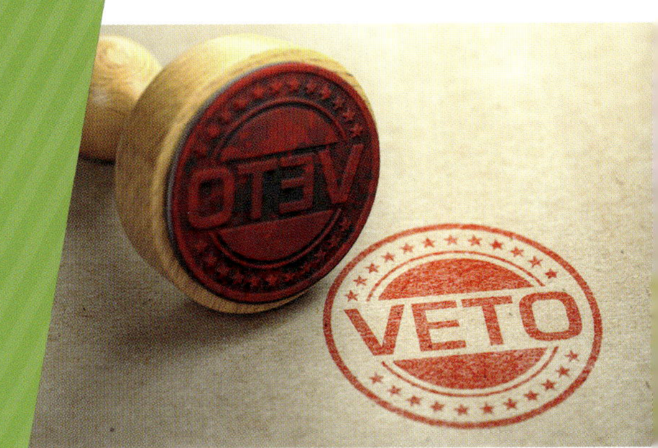

Lawmakers can vote "yea" or "nay," or yes or no, on bills, motions, and other issues.

WHO IS IN THE STATE LEGISLATURE?

The United States is a **democratic** republic. In this type of government, citizens vote for people to represent them. These representatives make the laws.

People who want to become state legislators share their ideas with voters. They talk to voters about their plans to make life better in the state.

This process is called a **campaign**. The person is called a **candidate**. At the end of the campaign, the state holds an election. The candidate who wins the most votes in his or her district becomes a state legislator.

In most states, the legislature is divided into two **chambers**. The first chamber is the **senate**. The second chamber is called the **house of representatives** in some states. It is called the assembly or house of delegates in others. There are always more state representatives than state senators.

Make a Guess!

When legislators run for office, they sometimes promise to vote for or against a certain law. What do you think would happen if they break that promise?

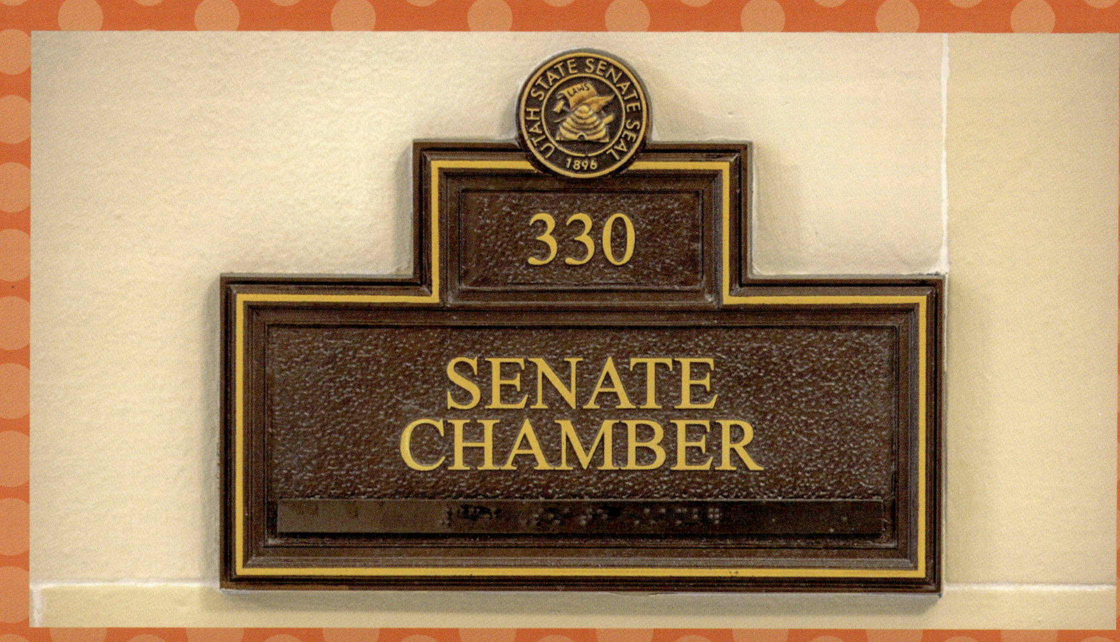
UTAH STATE SENATE SEAL
LABOR
1896
330
SENATE
CHAMBER

HOUSE OF REPRESENTATIVES
HOUSE OF REPRESENTATIVES
FLORIDA

The Michigan House of Representatives

Legislators in a state's house of representatives and senate keep each other in check. They balance each other to make sure neither one holds too much power.

Look!

All states have a legislature, but some are different from others. Some have a house of representatives. Others call it an assembly. Nebraska has one chamber instead of two. Examine your own state. What are the names and parts of your state's legislature?

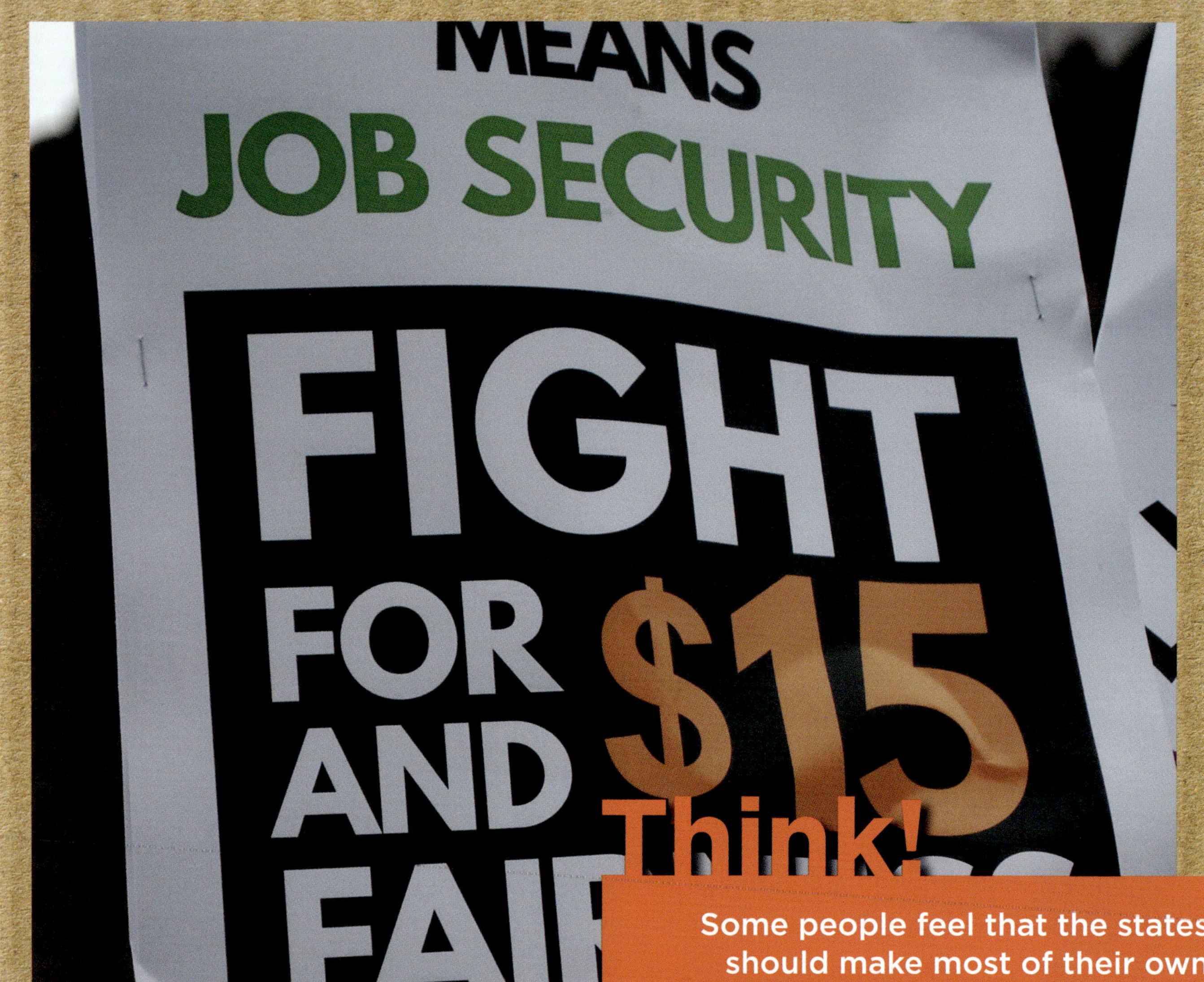

The federal minimum wage is set by the federal government. Some states set their own, higher, minimum wage.

Think!

Some people feel that the states should make most of their own laws. Other people think it's important for all states to follow the same laws. What do you think? Write down one reason that states should make their own laws. Then write one reason that states should follow national laws.

HOW DOES THE STATE LEGISLATURE AFFECT YOU?

Why does the state legislature matter? Because state laws can have a big impact on our lives. For example, Nebraska recently raised its minimum wage. In 2023, New York made it easier for its citizens to vote. These are just a few of the laws that might affect you in your state.

Other laws affect taxes, gun ownership, health care, and other parts of life.

Laws passed at the state level cannot be enforced in other states. But those laws can still affect the rest of the country. One state's laws can inspire other states' laws. This tells us that many people feel the same way about that idea. U.S. senators and representatives might notice this. They might then pass national laws. National laws apply to all states.

Ask Questions!

Remember, state legislators vote for or against new laws. Write a letter to your state senator and your representative. Ask them to tell you about a bill they voted for or against. Then ask them to explain why they voted as they did.

ACTIVITY

RESEARCH! Research your state. What is one new bill your state legislature passed this past year? Did the governor sign it into law? Talk with a partner about how this law might affect people in your state.

NEVADA STATE
LEGISLATURE

GLOSSARY

amended (uh-MEN-ded) changed

assembly (uh-SEM-blee) a gathering of people; a governmental body, especially a lower house of the legislature

campaign (kam-PAYN) the process of running for an elected position

candidate (KAN-duh-dayt) a person running for an elected government position

chambers (CHAYM-burz) sections of a legislature

debate (dih-BAYT) a discussion of an issue where participants present arguments for different sides

democratic (de-muh-KRAH-tik) describing a form of government in which people have a say in how they are governed

executive (ig-ZEH-kyoo-tiv) a government position holding the power to enforce laws

house of representatives (HOWS UHV reh-prih-ZEN-tuh-tivz) the larger of the two chambers in most state legislatures

judicial (joo-DIH-shul) relating to the branch of government that contains judges and courts

legislative (LE-juh-slay-tiv) related to the process of making laws

legislators (LE-juh-slay-tuhrz) elected representatives in charge of making laws

override (OH-vur-eyed) to set aside

senate (SEH-nuht) the smaller of the two chambers in most state legislatures

veto (VEE-toh) to stop a bill from becoming a law

FIND OUT MORE

Books

Bedesky, Baron. *What is a Government?* New York, NY: Crabtree Publishing Co., 2008.

Christelow, Eileen. *Vote!* New York, NY: Clarion Books, 2018.

Let's Go Local!: Role of Branches in Local Government in the US. Baby Professor, 2022.

Websites

Search these online sources with an adult.

Local Government for Kids | Miacademy Learning Channel | YouTube
Learn how local government works.

iCivics
Find out how you can be an informed and involved citizen.

INDEX

ABOUT THE AUTHOR

Kevin Winn is a children's book writer and researcher. He focuses on issues of racial justice and educational equity in his work. In 2020, Kevin earned his doctorate in Educational Policy and Evaluation from Arizona State University.